SECRET SUSSEX TEA TRAIL

A Guide to the Tea Shops of East and West Sussex

Joan Ellis and Pauline Cherry

S.B. Publications

We dedicate this book to our good friend Professor Sandra Humble-Johnson of Ohio who inspired us to set up Secret Sussex Tours Ltd saying 'give us tea shops', and to Ina Wishner who not only runs the Tea Cosy Tea Company but spends as much time as she can painting the Sussex landscape.

First published in 1997 by SB Publications
c/o 19 Grove Road, Seaford, East Sussex, BN25 1TP

ISBN 1 85770 107 0

Typeset by JEM Lewes and printed by
MPF Design and Print Ltd, 32 Thomas Street
Longford Trading Estate, Stratford, Greater Manchester M32 0JT.

CONTENTS

TEA MERCHANTS

4

INTRODUCTION

THIS guide to teashops in East and West Sussex is intended for all those whose pleasure in life is an afternoon of agreeable indulgence in delightful surroundings, enjoying a real English cream tea.

Joan Ellis and Pauline Cherry of Secret Sussex Tours Limited organise tours by coach around Sussex and, in response to many requests, have put their extensive knowledge of teashops into this little book.

When the sun shines is an obvious time to go for a tea trip, but in winter a visit to a beamed teashop where there is a roaring log fire can be just the tonic to lift the spirit.

A POTTED HISTORY

IT IS believed that the drink of tea was first discovered, by accident, in 3000BC. The Chinese Emperor Chen Nong was sitting in his garden sipping a bowl of hot water when the breeze blew some leaves into the vessel. He so enjoyed the flavour that he continued to have water with leaves served as a beverage and it was from this that our present cuppa has evolved. Tea became fashionable in England in the mid 17th century. It came from China on fast tea clippers, but was so expensive that only the rich could afford to buy tea. A local diary entry on October 8, 1714, reads: 'paid 4 shillings at Lewes for a quarter lb of tea' - this showing that it was by then widely available although not inexpensive. At about the same time Thomas Twining acquired a coffee house at the sign of the Golden Lion in the Strand, London, to sell tea. The beverage soon became so popular that he opened a shop next door to sell nothing other than loose tea.

The drinking of tea was said to be good for you; in fact in Scotland it was sold by apothecaries, and was available on prescription. The number of the prescription form was 99 — and this is the number now used by the Co-op as a brand name. Typhoo, another brand name, is Chinese for doctor.

When tea was a costly commodity, those looking to make a quick profit adulterated it by adding such things as dried sheeps' dung or ash tree leaves soaked in copperas. John Horniman addressed the problem by setting up a business on the Isle of Wight that packed tea in sealed packets thus preventing tampering and ensuring the correct weight.

Sussex, with its long coastline and navigable rivers, has a long history of smuggling, and among the contraband was tea. To avoid the high taxes imposed on tea, it was brought ashore illegally, packed in oil skins to keep it dry. Then it was carried over the Downs by packhorses that moved silently along the old tracks to avoid the excise men. The handlers were paid a 'dollop' of tea (40lb) for a night's work. In 1737 the Groombridge Gang was said to handle 3,000lb of tea a week, most of it disposed of in London. Stories abound of hiding places — secret rooms in chimneys, tunnels and under beehives — where no tax man would look. It was not until 1784, when the tax on tea was reduced, that smuggling of tea was brought to a halt.

Anna, Duchess of Bedford, is credited with the start of the tradition of afternoon tea about 1840. She often became peckish at around 4pm in the afternoon and, deciding to introduce a new meal between the midday and evening meals, she invited friends to share dainty little sandwiches, cakes and cups of tea.

Surprisingly, ye olde tea rooms are not that olde. They came about towards the end of the 19th century when cycling in the countryside became popular, and when the first cars were seen on the roads. Country folk opened their doors to people cycling or motoring out from the towns, offering them a pot of tea or home made lemonade, scones and a slice of cake. From this humble beginning has grown the tea rooms we know today.

A NATION OF TEA DRINKERS

TEA is the favourite beverage in Britain, accounting for 43 per cent of all we drink, including coffee, alcohol and milk. Of the 70 per cent of regular tea drinkers in Britain, 95 per cent add milk and 63 per cent do not take sugar. On average everyone over the age of ten drinks four cups of tea a day. It is estimated that the total amount of cups of tea drunk in a day in the British Isles is 175 million.

ALFRISTON

BADGERS
13 North Street
Alfriston
East Sussex

Telephone: 01323 870849
Open: Daily 11am to 6pm all year
Proprietor: Mike Thatcher
Parking: West Street and The Willows car parks

Alfriston is a splendid old village of great character. Wander around the quaint streets, stroll along the river bank and discover the church known as the Cathedral of the Downs, and its neighbour, the Clergy House (open to the public and the first building owned by the National Trust. It was bought in 1896 for £10). The High Street, with its half timbered inns and shops, and its ancient market cross, provides some splendid subjects for artists and photographers. Look for the old lock up in West Street car park.

Badgers is a 16th century tea house popular with the tourists. Its appeal is in the small beamed rooms that are cosy in winter and cool in the heat of a summer's day. The food is very good and vegetarians are well catered for.

A real treat for a special occasion is Badger's Champagne Tea, which consists of chilled champagne followed by smoked salmon sandwiches, egg and cress sandwiches (or your own choice of sandwiches), scone with jam and cream and a cake to follow (if you have room for it). You need to book two hours ahead so that the champagne can be put on ice. Badger's cream teas are delicious, with banana and walnut cake, and bacon and stilton toasties being specialities.

Badgers is open all year, although Mike closes occasionally on a Wednesday for maintenance.

AMBERLEY

Amberley Castle Hotel
Amberley
West Sussex

Telephone:	01798 831991
Open:	Daily, but ring for reservation
Proprietors:	Joy and Martin Cummings
Parking:	On site

Amberley is one of the most delightful villages in Sussex. Its picturesque houses and cottages have been a favourite subject for artists over the centuries. This is a lovely, peaceful spot for walkers on the South Downs Way to stop, rest and admire the beautiful Wild Brooks with their unique birds, plants and wildlife.

Amberley Castle, now a country house hotel, dates from the 12th century, when the original manor house was built by Bishop Luffa. The castle is surrounded by well maintained gardens where white peacocks bring their opulence and stately splendour to the grounds.

Tea is taken in one of several reception rooms all of which are beautifully furnished. Guests are seated on sumptuous sofas or armchairs with low tea tables elegantly laid out with bone china, pots of clotted cream and strawberry jam, and napkins folded like dicky shirts with knives and pastry forkes tucked into them. A large pot of freshly made tea arrives and you are invited to help yourself (and they mean it) to an assortment of daintily cut sandwiches and an amazing selection of scones and cakes.

There is a fixed price per person for tea, and although not cheap, it was probably the best value for money we encountered in Sussex. Reservations must be made in advance.

ARUNDEL

Dominating this elegant Georgian town's skyline are two enormous buildings - the castle, with its huge stone outer walls abutting the High Street, and the Roman Catholic Cathedral of St Philip Neri. The steep High Street has an old coaching inn, a toy and military museum and some interesting little shops. At the bottom of the town the tree lined road runs alongside the river to Swanbourne boating lake and the nearby Arundel Wildfowl reserve.

The original castle was built by the Normans to guard the gap in the Downs where the Arun flows through to the sea. It was destroyed in the Civil War and lay in ruins for many years. Piecemeal restoration began in 1718 but the castle we see today was mainly the work of Henry, 15th Duke of Norfolk, who inherited in 1860 at the age of thirteen. The castle is open from Easter until October and closed on Saturdays.

It is at Arundel Castle that the first cricket match is often played between visiting touring teams and the Duke of Norfolk's eleven before the series for the Test Matches.

Between the castle and town is the church of St Nicholas which dates from 1380. This is believed by many to be the best building in Arundel. It was amicably shared by Catholics and Anglicans until a row over ownership, after which a brick wall was built to divide the chancel from the nave. The entrance from the street is to the Church of England section while from the castle there is access to the Roman Catholic side. A glass screen now replaces the brick wall.

Arundel Cathedral, a more recent addition to the town, stands on

9

concrete foundations 50ft deep. JA Hansom (inventor of the Hansom cab) designed it in the medieval style, and work began in 1869. A small spire crowns the vast roof and a feature of the west front is a magnificent rose window.

Belinda's Restaurant
Tarrant Street
Arundel
West Sussex

Telephone: 01903 882977
Open: *Tuesday-Friday 9.30am-5.30pm*
              Saturday 9.30am-5.30pm
              Sunday 11am-5.30pm
Parking: *Nearby*

Belinda's Restaurant is set in a famous 16th century building in Tarrant Street. It has an instant appeal to the visitor with its white weatherboarding and black paintwork set off by pretty hanging baskets in the summer. The windows are always full of wonderfully enticing goodies and during the winter months there is a lovely cosy atmosphere with a roaring fire in the hearth. The cakes are so delicious that it is difficult to make a choice, and there are wonderful smells of warm bread wafting around from the bakehouse. Belinda's specialises in English home cooked food, home made cakes and desserts. Specialities include bakewell tart, treacle tart and cheesecake. To drink, there is a good assortment of teas such as Earl Grey, Assam, Darjeeling, herbal teas and fruit teas.

The Copper Kettle
21 Tarrant Street
Arundel
West Sussex

Telephone: 01903 883679
Owners: *Geoffrey and Carol Squire*
Parking: *Nearby*

The Copper Kettle is an enchanting teashop set in an interesting timber framed Tudor building with a jettied front, the only surviving example of its age in the town. Lunches are served from noon and last orders are taken at 4.30pm. Specialities are the Copper Kettle's salads, which are all beautifully served.

The staff are friendly and efficient and the waitresses wear long, pale green frilled pinnies, which look very quaint. The food is good and wholesome. Prices are average and portions are ample. The Arundel cream tea provides a pot of tea or cup of filter coffee with home made scones, butter, jam and whipped double cream. Also available is a variety of cakes and pastries. Assam, Ceylon, Darjeeling and Earl Grey teas are available, and there are good coffees, including decaffeinated, and hot chocolate topped with whipped cream.

BATTLE

Gateway Tea Rooms
78 High Street
Battle
East Sussex

Telephone: 01424 772856
Open: Every day
Owner: Ruth Reeve

October 14 1066 is the one date that sticks in everyone's mind from school days. On that day King Harold was cut down by a Norman sword and William of Normandy claimed the throne of England. In 1070 William founded Battle Abbey to atone for the slaughter, placing the high altar at the spot where Harold died. The impressive medieval Great Abbey Gatehouse stands at the south end of Battle High Street.English Heritage administers the Abbey remains, which are open to the public.

Just opposite the Great Gatehouse is Gateway Tea Rooms (and licensed restaurant). It is furnished with oak chairs and tables to complement the old beams and lanterns hang on the walls. The friendly service and home cooking make this a welcoming place to relax after a visit to the Abbey or a look around the shops and the nearby Yesterday's World museum. The wonderful cream cakes and pastries are displayed in a cool cabinet at the rear of the shop. Outsize chocolate eclairs are extremely popular as are the house speciality of clotted cream teas. Traditional Sunday lunches are served as well as snacks and sandwiches. On summer days meals may be eaten in the garden.

BEXHILL

The Walnut Tree Tea Rooms
6 High Street
Old Town
Bexhill
East Sussex

Telephone: 01424 223797
Open: 10am-5pm Tuesday to Saturday, 11am-3pm
   Sunday
Parking: At the garden car park.

Bexhill Old Town, often passed through without a second glance, is a fascinating cluster of old houses, shops and an inn.

In 1968 a manor house was mainly demolished to enable the road to be widened, and its remains have been magically transformed into a public garden. The former rooms, planted in various designs, are approached through the old doorways that lead into the secret gardens beyond. The manor barn still exists and is now used to house the Museum of Costume and Social History.

This small tea room, which takes its name from a very large walnut tree that once grew on the site, has been given the Heartbeat Award for its wholesome food and spotless premises.

The teas here are very reasonably priced, as are the lunches. The

12

home made cakes are displayed on a table at the rear of the shop enabling you to have a good look before you choose. There is a selection of rock cakes, scones, small fairy cakes and slices of fruit and seed cake, and if you want to take some home they will sell you whole cakes.

The lunches are all carefully thought out with the emphasis on healthy eating. Puddings include eleven flavours of ice cream.

BILLINGSHURST

Burdocks
59 High Street
Billingshurst
West Sussex

Telephone: 01403 782750
Owner: Debbie Dawtrey
Open: Daily 9.30am-5.30pm
(subject to seasonal variations)
Parking: Library car park in lane opposite

Billingshurst is a charming small town of picturesque period properties, on the A264 six miles south west of Horsham. The name Billingshurst is thought to derive from Belinus, the Roman who laid out Stane Street.

The open fire in this old oak beamed tea shop gives a warm cosy atmosphere in which to enjoy a pot of tea. There is an old bread oven, the walls are hung with photographs of Billingshurst in years past and hop vines decorate the beams. Burdocks is a very pleasant place to take a break.

A side table groans with any array of delectable goodies and hand made cakes of all types to tempt the palate. Each day brings something different but there is usually an extremely good fruit cake, a delicious sticky chocolate cake and a bakewell tart among the others on offer.

Tea blends include China and Indian.

13

BODIAM

Bodiam Castle

Knollys
Bodiam
East Sussex

Telephone: 01580 830232
Open: Daily 10.30am-5pm, Easter until mid October
Parking: Outside or at castle

A fairy tale castle really is built at the bottom of the garden here at Knollys. Bodiam Castle, owned by the National Trust, stands majestically in the centre of a large moat that reflects the ancient walls amid the waterlilies. Although only the exterior is intact the castle is fascinating for both children and adults alike. There are spiral staircases to climb, battlements to walk around and wonderful views over the surrounding countryside. The castle was built in 1385 as a defence against a French invasion that never happened. Bodiam is off the B2244 between Hawkhurst and Staplecross.

Knollys is just the place to rest after looking around the castle or to visit while out for a drive in the country. The choice of teas includes Assam, China, Darjeeling and Earl Grey, and to eat there are freshly baked cream cakes and sponges and excellent salmon and cucumber sandwiches. Knollys also has a good gift shop, a lovely garden to sit in on warm days and sometimes there are plants for sale.

BOSHAM

The waters of Chichester Harbour lap against the quayside of this outstandingly beautiful village, creeping over the top at high tide and flooding the little roads. All the old houses have high steps in front of their door to keep the water at bay. The sea has always played an important role here. St Wilfrid came to Sussex in 681, landing at Bosham, to convert the population to Christianity. He was dismayed to find the residents in great distress as a drought had caused their crops to fail and the cattle to die. Some people were even throwing themselves into the sea to drown rather than face starvation. St Wilfrid taught them how to fish by casting nets into the sea, providing themselves with food.

Another notable resident was King Canute, who was so venerated by his loyal subjects that they claimed he could hold back the tide of the sea. To prove that he was a mere mortal he had his throne placed on the sands and there he sat until the tide brought the water in, washing around him, thus making his point.

The church tower and chancel are Saxon. At the end of the last century workmen repairing the floor came across an old tomb containing the remains of an eight year old child. Legend claims the child was Canute's daughter.

King Harold came to pray at the church before setting sail for France in 1064. The events that followed led to the invasion by William of Normandy in 1066, and Bosham church is depicted on the Bayeux Tapestry.

Mariners Coffee Shop
1 High Street
Old Bosham
West Sussex PO18 8LS

Telephone: 01243 572960
Open: All year 10.30am-5.30p
        except Christmas Day
Owners: Jayne Checkley and Penelope Ware

Here is the only tea room we have visited where sea laps the outside walls at high tide. Swans wait patiently outside the bay window to be fed.

The cakes are mainly of the extra gooey type with the famous Sussex Banoffee Pie (born at the Hungry Monk, Jevington) a firm favourite. There are also scones and extra large sponge sandwiches and gateaux. At lunch time there are daily specials plus soups, fish dishes and jacket potatoes with various fillings like prawns. Fish is extremely fresh as it is sold on the quay outside the shop.

Be warned by signs saying not to park on the shore; many have returned to find their cars in the water.

BRIGHTON

The Royal Pavilion has been home to three British monarchs. It was built for George IV when he was The Prince Regent, and was also used by his brother William IV, and their niece, Victoria, who was not terribly enamoured of it. It began as a farmhouse; in 1787 architect Henry Holland created a neo-classical villa on the site and it was later transformed into an Indian style palace, with domes and minarets, by John Nash between 1815 and 1822. Although it is a folly, and a bizarre mix of Indian palace, chinoiserie and a touch of Saracen, the Royal Pavilion is a unified entity, made so by the brilliant imagination of its creator, the Prince Regent. It is a magical place to visit, full of astonishing works of art, brilliant colours, superb craftsmanship and opulent extravagance beyond words.

The pavilion offers many services, such as guided tours, educational facilities for those with special needs, hire of the state rooms and wedding ceremonies. The Pavilion shop has carefully chosen books, prints, ceramics, exquisite jewellery and reproductions of the Pavilion's own wallpapers and fabrics.

The Queen Adelaide Tea Rooms
The Royal Pavilion
Brighton

Open: Daily (except December 25 and 26)
June to September 10am-6pm
October to May 10am to 5pm

The tea rooms in The Royal Pavilion are the ideal retreat to sit and rest in after browsing around the magnificent interior of Prinny's Palace. Enjoy a Regency tea or a light lunch overlooking the sweeping views of the newly restored gardens. These tea rooms are elegant, beautifully kept and with very friendly and efficient staff to serve you. The cakes are a wondrous size and prices are reasonable.

The Mock Turtle
4 Pool Valley
Brighton
East Sussex

Telephone: 01273 327380
Open: 10am-6pm. Tuesday to Saturday
Owners: Mr and Mrs Chater

Pool Valley was once a small harbour used by the local fisherman. Gradually it silted up leaving the little shops that had once been on the quayside some distance from the water's edge. The Mock Turtle is one of those shops. Old pictures show boats tossed about like corks during storms in the valley that is now the bus station.

The Mock Turtle is a very popular meeting place, and customers spill out into the street in warm weather. Oak furniture and fresh flowers on the tables greet the eye when you enter this old fashioned tea shop. Here all the delicious cakes and breads are made on the premises and the scones, served fresh from the oven, melt in your mouth. The kitchen is situated on the first floor, allowing all manner of aromas to waft down to the shop, tempting the hungry to indulge in the excellent fare. Fruit cakes, chocolate cake, doughnuts, meringues and gateaux vie for a place in the window and on the display table. There is a good selection of teas to choose from, and coffee. A tempting range of lunch time savoury snacks, such as welsh rarebit. are also available, and there is a takeaway service as well.

BURWASH

Built along a ridge in the high Weald between the Rother and Dudwell rivers, Burwash High Street boasts an extremely attractive line of old houses, cottages, shops and inns. It was once important in the days when the Weald produced most of England's iron ore. It is a broad, picturesque street, lined with pollarded trees. Legend says that when a Roman garrison marched through the area, Bur, the soldiers' dog, became weighed down by the mud on the road to the extent that he could travel no further. On reaching a river it was decided to wash the mud off poor Bur - hence the name Burwash.

The Back Parlour
Just So
High Street
Burwash
East Sussex

Telephone:	*01435 883541*
Open:	*Monday to Saturday*
	9am-5pm, Sunday 10am-4.30pm
Owners:	*Peter and Lavinia Giles*
Parking:	*In free public car park opposite*

The Back Parlour is well named as it is just that. After threading your way through an Aladdin's cave packed with fascinating goods of all kinds you descend into the tea shop. Even the walls here are jam packed with an array of edible delights such as decorative bottles of flavoured oil, jars of unusual spices, salts that look as though they were collected at Alum Bay in the days when you could scrape the coloured sands from the cliffs into glass containers, Turkish teas, chocolates, biscuits, jams and preserves. The sign on the wall says that there are 130 different varieties of edible items in stock and we were sure there were probably more.

Teas on offer include traditional English, Ceylon, Darjeeling and lemon tea, also a variety of herbal teas such as fennel and lemon balm, peppermint and rosehip and hibiscus. There are home made cakes and gateaux, pastries and biscuits, and toasted teacakes. Hot cheese scone or hot croissant with strawberry preserve may be ordered. For lunch, savoury hot cheese and onion pasties, cream of spinach pastie or toasted cheese muffin are on offer at reasonable prices.

The Tea Room
Bateman's
Burwash
East Sussex

Telephone: 01435 882302
Open: April to end October, Saturday to Wednesday 11am-5.30pm, plus Good Friday
Owner: The National Trust
Parking: Car park

In 1634 an ironmaster built Bateman's House in a peaceful valley where the river Dudwell flows. The gabled house with its towering chimney stacks has mellowed with the passing of time and is set in beautifully kept, tranquil gardens. Bateman's was the home of Rudyard Kipling from 1902 to 1936. The house has been kept as it was in his lifetime.

At 2pm on Saturday afternoons the working watermill is in operation grinding corn. Here Kipling installed water driven turbines to provide electricity for the house.

The tea room is in a long low building with a terrace at the back that opens into a sheltered garden where tables and chairs are set. Staff wear mob caps and frilly pinnies and the food is served on substantial stoneware crockery. Bateman's Special Tea provides cucumber sandwiches, scone, fruit cake and pot of tea for one, while the Sussex Cream Tea has two scones, cream, jam and pot of tea. Savoury snacks available include soup, jacket potatoes, Cornish pasties and daily specials.

Bateman's is on the A265 half a mile south of Burwash.

CHAILEY

May Cottage Tea Rooms
Haywards Heath Road
North Chailey
East Sussex

Telephone: 01825 724150
Open: Tuesday to Sunday 10am-6pm
Owner: Jill Noel
Parking: At rear

This delightful tea room is at the cross-roads of the A272 and the A275 almost opposite the Kings Head pub. The walls of the tea room are adorned with old sheet music and programmes of bygone musical events which bring back nostalgic memories of well loved tunes from the past. It is fascinating to sit and read the 'writing on the wall' as you wait for your order.

The speciality of the house is the excellent carrot cake, but also there are other delights to choose from such as the cream tea which comprises two scones, cream, strawberry jam and pot of tea.

Excellent, reasonably priced and satisfying hot meals are available at lunch time. They vary each day and are listed on the noticeboard.

The tea room is close to Chailey Common, where there are delightful walks through bracken and heather, with the sweet smell of the gorse in season. Also nearby is Chailey Windmill, which is open on Sundays and bank holidays. The smock mill is said to stand at the exact centre of Sussex. It fell idle in 1911 but has now found a new lease of life as a museum of rural life.

CUCKFIELD

Seasons
High Street
Cuckfield
West Sussex

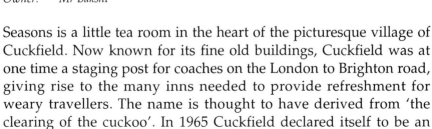

Telephone: 01444 457030
Open: 10am-4pm Monday to Saturday
Owner: Mr Bakshi

Seasons is a little tea room in the heart of the picturesque village of Cuckfield. Now known for its fine old buildings, Cuckfield was at one time a staging post for coaches on the London to Brighton road, giving rise to the many inns needed to provide refreshment for weary travellers. The name is thought to have derived from 'the clearing of the cuckoo'. In 1965 Cuckfield declared itself to be an 'independent state' with its own mayor.

The cakes are wonderful here, scones are large with ample portions of butter, jam and cream if desired. The cooking is superb and much thought is given to make the meals well presented and special. Seasons serves a very good scrambled egg with smoked salmon on toast at lunch time.

The sweet selection is 'yummy and naughty', all very rich, but there is a good fruit pie for those who prefer a plainer dessert. Seasons also sells superb Belgian chocolates.

DITCHLING

Stoneywish Country Park Tea Room
Spatham Lane (off B2116)
Ditchling
East Sussex

Telephone: 01273 843498/845471
Open: *Summer, seven days a week, 10am-7pm*
Parking: *Car park.*

Stoneywish Country Park is the ideal place for a family day out. A country walk takes visitors from the car park to a large picnic and play area with lovely views of Ditchling Beacon, and on to the Farm Centre where the original flint farm buildings now house an exhibition on rural life from the old days and local history.

There are also craft workshops, a working artist studio and a tea shop serving tasty home cooking at very reasonable prices. The soups are excellent and the bread rolls delicious. Various tempting cakes of all sorts are available.

While you enjoy your meal a variety of birds and animals wander around outside and there is a Pets corner which has baby animals for children to see and touch.

Disabled access to almost all parts of the park is possible by wheelchair, and arrangements can be made for access to the tea shop by the back entrance if necessary (telephone ahead). Disabled WCs are situated in the Farm Centre.

DUDDLESWELL

Duddleswell Tea Rooms
Duddleswell
Ashdown Forest
East Sussex

Telephone: 01825 712126
Open: 10am-5pm Bank holiday
Mondays; Tuesday to
Sunday, February to
November; 10am-4pm
Friday to Sunday, December and January.
Closed Christmas and New Year for two weeks
Owners: Geff and Debby Lowe
Parking: Car park

This is a well known tea shop on beautiful Ashdown Forest - on the B2026. It is renowned for its quality and friendly service, and here you can rekindle memories of childhood with such delicacies as Marmite soldiers. All the food is well prepared and nicely present-ed, making the home made cakes, light lunches and afternoon teas very tempting.

There is a Senior Citizens' Happy Hour (10am to 11am Tuesday to Friday) when a pot of coffee with a choice of scone, fruit cake or anything toasted may be ordered for just £1.80. Lunch is served between noon and 2pm. You can often sit outside on sunny winter days, as well as sun worship in the summer.

One thing to beware of is crossing the road from the car park to the tea shop as the traffic flies along this road.

EASTBOURNE

The Pavilion Tea Rooms
Royal Parade
Eastbourne
East Sussex

Telephone: 01323 410374
Open: Daily 9am to 5.30pm (9pm in summer)
Parking: On sea front and nearby roads

If you are looking for a genteel atmosphere and a glimpse of how life was lived in the past you are in for a very pleasant surprise if you visit The Pavilion, which is decorated in the Edwardian style,

and has a resident pianist who plays such pieces as Lilac Time and Perchance to Dream during the afternoons and evenings. Tea can also be taken on the terrace or in the sun lounge where the daily newspapers are provided for customers. The whole effect is of the gracious charm and elegance of a bygone era.

Tea from the leaf is served in beautiful china teapots with drip catchers attached, and little tea strainers. There is an excellent choice of cakes and fancies together with cinnamon toast and crumpets, all well presented on the delicate china. Prices are not cheap but for the pleasure of using such elegant surroundings and enjoying a well served cream tea, it is really worth every penny. Within the tea rooms is a charming little shop that sells all types of tea and everything connected with it, such as teapots, tea towels, strainers, drip catchers and many other items.

EAST HOATHLY

Clara's Coffee Shop
9 High Street
East Hoathly
East Sussex

Telephone: 01825 840339
Open: 10.30am-5pm Wednesday to Saturday
2pm to 5pm Sundays and Bank Holidays
Owner: Jane Seabrook

Local diarist Thomas Turner has left a fascinating account of life in East Hoathly in the mid 1700s. A draper with a weakness for drink, he tells of many drunken escapades not least among them being the night he became so intoxicated with a group of friends that he dressed in his wife's petticoats and danced on the bed. No doubt he got a good wigging from his wife Peggy who tried to keep him on the straight and narrow.

Clara's Coffee Shop in the High Street is set in an old, well kept building. Jane has her modern farmhouse kitchen in the middle of the shop so customers can watch her make the cakes and fill the rolls. There is a tempting choice of shortbreads, sponges and toasted tea cakes to indulge in with a pot of tea, or home made soup, filled rolls and a side salad for lunch.

The shop has another side that sells books at reasonable prices, antiques and bric-a-brac. Upstairs is a large range of Rowan knitting yarns and haberdashery in the beamed gallery. There is also an exhibition of old knitting patterns and memorabilia.

EXCEAT

Exceat Farmhouse
Exceat
Nr Seaford
East Sussex

Telephone: 01323 870218
Open: Daily
Owner: Sally Davis
Parking: At rear

Set at the edge of Friston Forest in the Severn Sisters Country Park is an old house now used as a tea shop and restaurant. Inside are whitewashed walls, old beams hung with hop bines, pine furniture and Liberty print curtains, making this farmhouse style kitchen a pleasant place to enjoy a break after walking through the woods or along the banks of the river Cuckmere down to the sea. On fine days there is a courtyard full of tables and chairs where you

ADDENDUM
Page 26.
Please note that
since publication this
teashop has closed.

can eat al fresco.

There is an excellent variety of home made cakes, with the selection changing daily, as well as the cream tea which comprises two scones, jam, cream and with a pot of Sussex tea. The range of teas includes Kenya, China, Darjeeling, Earl Grey and Sussex.

At lunch time there is a good selection of light snacks as well as full meals. In the evenings gourmet theme nights are arranged, such as a Pudding Night where as many as a dozen different desserts are served. To check for details and dates ring Mrs Davis. Parties and corporate entertaining can also be arranged.

FALMER

Falmer Stores Tea Room
Mill Street
Falmer
East Sussex

Telephone: 01273 604157
Open: 10am-4pm Monday to Saturday;
Wednesday 10am-2pm
Owners: Linda and Andrew Bolingbroke

The small village of Falmer, now split in two by the A27, is monopolised by the ever encroaching Universities of Brighton and Sussex, but it has stood its ground, retaining its pub and quaint store with post office and tea room combined. Linda, Andrew and their assistant Val are extremely helpful and friendly people always greeting you with a smile and ready to serve in the shop or wait on table. Sweet jars line the shelves with such favourites as humbugs or rhubarb and custard, mint balls and lemon sherbets. Tiny wooden drawers hold all sorts of things from soap to sugar while on the counter sits a charmingly ornate old fashioned till. Fresh eggs are available from the Bolingbrokes own chickens and the fruit and vegetables are locally grown.

The tea shop is pleasantly old fashioned and has a glowing coal fire in a small iron grate warming the room in winter. It is popular with students from the universities and hikers walking the South Downs Way. The daily menu is written on a blackboard and the dishes are reasonably priced. Cakes are all home made with the portions being generous. In summer visitors are welcome to sit in the secluded garden under the shade of the trees.

FIRLE

Firle Place
Firle
East Sussex
BN8 6LP

Telephone: 01273 858335
Open: 2p-5pm June to September, Wednesdays,
              Thursdays and Sundays; also Easter and
              bank holiday Mondays
Owner: Viscount Gage
Parking: Adjacent to house

Firle Place shelters in a fold of the South Downs beneath the 718ft high Firle Beacon in a beautiful parkland setting. It has been the home of the Gage family for more than 500 years, when Eleanor St Clere brought her estate at Heighton St Clere with her on her marriage to John Gage. Sir John Gage (1479-1556) who had been governor of Calais, Vice Chamberlain to Henry VIII and Constable of the Tower of London, built the Tudor manor house from Caen stone. The present facade was remodelled in the 18th century. Firle is still very much a family home and its elegant proportions provide a perfect setting for important collections of furniture, Sevres porcelain and internationally renowned Old Masters. The memorabilia of General Thomas Gage (and his wife Margaret Kemble of New Jersey) who was commander in chief of the British forces in America at the outbreak of the War of Independence brings many American visitors to the house.

The terrace of this lovely house, with its views over the park and lake, is one of the most idyllic places to take tea or a cold buffet lunch. During inclement weather you may enjoy eating in the licensed restaurant under the portraits of members of the Gage dynasty. Lunches are served from noon and teas from 3pm.

GORING BY SEA

Cynthia's Tea Rooms
14 Sea Place
Goring by Sea
Worthing
West Sussex

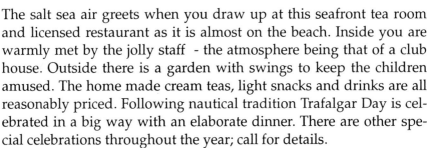

Telephone: 01903 242119
Open: February 1 to December 25
Parking: Outside; disabled access; dogs welcome

The salt sea air greets when you draw up at this seafront tea room and licensed restaurant as it is almost on the beach. Inside you are warmly met by the jolly staff - the atmosphere being that of a club house. Outside there is a garden with swings to keep the children amused. The home made cream teas, light snacks and drinks are all reasonably priced. Following nautical tradition Trafalgar Day is celebrated in a big way with an elaborate dinner. There are other special celebrations throughout the year; call for details.

Sea Lane Cafe
Marine Crescent
Goring by Sea
West Sussex

Telephone: 01903 247847
Owners: P and E Stubbs
Open: Eight a week (their description)

This seafront cafe calls itself 'the not yet world famous cafe' but many of its regular visitors from all over the world feel the Stubbs are underestimating themselves. Its cakes are talked about world wide as are its sea food dishes. If you are on a diet don't look at the cakes and pastries they are so tempting, with cream slices the size of house bricks, strawberry tarts full to the brim and glazed over and enormous chocolate eclairs. The drinks list is long and varied with children being well catered for.

HAILSHAM

The Homely Maid
2 High Street
Hailsham
East Sussex

Telephone: 01323 841650
Owner: Peter Broyd
Open: Monday to Friday 9am to 5pm, Saturday
9am to 2pm
Parking: Car park at rear of shopping centre

Amid the bustle of this busy market town is a haven of peace and comfort where you can rest weary feet and meet friends to enjoy a quick snack, lunch or a steaming bowl of delicious home made soup served with chunky bread or an excellent cream tea. Loose tea is always used at the Homely Maid with tea strainers provided with

each pot of tea. The whole atmosphere is that of comings and goings, people greeting each other and catching up on gossip over a cup of tea.

The Homely Maid lives up to its name having a homely cottage ambience with friendly and helpful staff. Prices are reasonable and the service is good

Pies, bread and cakes may be bought in the Homely Maid's shop.

HASTINGS

Katie's Pantry
George Street
Old Town
Hastings

Telephone: 01424 425821
Owner: Ruth Parsons
Open: 11am-5.30pm (6.30pm in July
and August)
Parking: On seafront

To find this 17th century tea shop you must go to Old Town where the tall black net drying huts stand on the beach and two Victorian cliff lifts climb West and East Hills. George Street runs parallel to the seafront and as it is pedestrianised it is possible to amble along looking at the shops in safety. There are gift shops, craft shops, book shops and a fascinating old fashioned hardware shop that seems to stock everything from a tin bath to a broom.

Katie's Pantry is easily spotted by its lattice windows and small step that leads to the entrance door. Inside you will be charmed by the old beams, oak tables and chairs laid with pretty china and walls bedecked with fishing nets and pictures of old Hastings.

There are 14 types of luxury loose tea available including Piccadilly, Irish Breakfast and Russian Caravan and the same number of herbal fruit teas, some of which are fennel, apple and cinnamon and nettle and wild cherry. A sideboard groans under the display of home made cakes.

Unique to Katie's Pantry is the Sussex Cheese Tea comprising two home made wholemeal scones with butter, mature cheddar cheese, apple, pickle and pot of tea. Another set tea is Fruit Cream Tea, consisting of two fruit scones, Cornish clotted cream, blackcurrant or strawberry jam with pot of tea. The Healthy Honey Tea is made up of two scones, Greek yoghurt, honey and pot of tea.

HENFIELD

**Norton House
High Street
Henfield**

Telephone: 01273 492064
Open: Monday,Thursday, Friday, Saturday
*   9.30am-5.30pm; Sunday 10am-12.30pm*
*   and 3pm-5.30pm*
Owners: Mr and Mrs Sinclair-Young
Parking: At rear in free car park; disabled access

This tea shop was a joint winner of the Top Tea Shop Of The Year for 1995 awarded by the Tea Council. It has all the right ingredients that give delight to tea buffs - a relaxed atmosphere, old beams, oak tables and chairs.

The tea used is always in leaf form. Jean Sinclair-Young has never used a tea bag and vows she never will and her home made cakes are a delight. Norton House is renowned for its rock cakes and Christmas mince pies.

Another tradition that Jean keeps alive is the childhood favourite of the boiled egg tea which is still as popular as ever. Cream teas are made up of two scones, butter, jam and cream with a pot of tea. There is a choice of teas on offer including Assam, China, Earl Grey, Lapsang, Keemun, and Darjeeling. On warm days tea can be taken in the pretty garden at the rear of the shop. There is also an interesting gift shop attached.

KIRDFORD

**Russets Tea Room
Kirdford Growers
Kirdford
Nr Billinghurst
West Sussex**

Telephone: 01403 820003
Open: Wednesday to
*   Sunday 10am-5pm*
Owner: Pauline Stevens
Parking: On site

  Russets Tea Room is set within the complex of the Kirdford Growers shopping facility. To find Russets take the Billinghurst to Petworth road (A272) turning off at Wisborough Green then follow the signs to Kirdford. The tea room is quite large, seating 50-55 people, and coach parties are welcome. Around the room there are several stands selling an assortment of antiques, bric-a-brac and craft items, making interesting browsing.

The delicious home made cakes are temptingly displayed on a table giving quite a choice including coffee and walnut cake, chocolate, Russets apple cake and the house speciality, farmhouse fruit cake. Or you may prefer a toasted tea cake, or a cream tea with two scones, butter, jam, cream and a cup of tea. Tea varieties include Earl Grey, English Breakfast and lemon and for coffee lovers there is Douwe Egburts and Rombouts.

The Kirdford Growers run a thriving fruit farm that has been established for about a century. The many varieties of apples and pears produced here can be bought in the farm shop, as well as apple juice, local cheeses, wines, cooked meats and farm produce.

LEWES

Lewes, the county town of East Sussex, has a history predating Saxon times. Following the Norman Conquest of 1066 William allocated Lewes to his nobleman William de Warrene, whose wife, Gundrada, was thought to be the Conqueror's daughter. The de Warrenes built Lewes Castle, a double motte and bailey fortification, and they also founded a great priory, dedicated to St Pancras, which became the mother house of the Cluniac order in England. Both castle and priory are now in ruins - the first through neglect, and the propensity of the townsfolk to take the castle stones to build their own homes; the second through the Dissolution of the Monasteries. Both are open the public.

Close to the priory remains in Southover is Anne of Cleves House, given as part of her divorce settlement to Henry VIII's Flemish wife. The house is now a museum.

The town is well known as an antiques centre. Here are six multi-stall antiques centres, a number of individual shops, bustling flea markets and three prestigious auction rooms.

White Hart Hotel
High Street
Lewes
East Sussex

Telephone: *01273 473794*
Open: *Daily*
Owners: *Mr and Mrs C Ayris*
Parking: *In town car parks*

This old coaching inn dating back to the 16th century stands opposite the Law Courts in the High Street. It has a Georgian facade to a much older building. Inside there is a comfortable feel to the well used rooms that contain a wealth of beams.

Tea or coffee can be taken in the inner lounge where rattan arm-chairs with padded seats are arranged around low tables that invite you to tarry over tea as you are warmed by the large black iron stove. In good weather there is a roof patio with views to Newhaven and the sea. The White Hart Cream Tea consists of a pot of tea, two scones, butter, jam and freshly whipped cream , and the Sussex Tea comprises a pot of tea with toasted tea cake, butter and jam. French Coffee provides a croissant, jam and a pot of coffee. On the trolley are fresh cream cakes and pastries.

Between 1768 and 1774 Lewes resident Thomas Paine established the Headstrong Club in the White Hart. Here issues of the day were debated, and Paine often won an award for being the 'most obstinate haranguer'. He had come to Lewes as an excise officer, taking lodgings at Bull House, a tobacconist shop in the High Street. He married his landlord's daughter, and for a time he ran the shop himself, but his mind was on greater things and soon he abandoned his family and left for North America where his revolutionary ideas helped free the colonists from the yoke of British imperialism.

Lewes is famous around the world for its November 5 Bonfire, an occasion that commemorates not only the Gunpowder Plot, but also the martyrdom of local Protestants during the Marian persecutions. Magnificent torchlight processions wind through the narrow streets from early evening to midnight, and there are five fire sites where massive bonfires are lit, 'archbishops' harangue the crowds and spectacular fireworks displays are staged. During the evening flaming tar barrels are cast into the River Ouse, and the old town resounds to the music of a dozen or more bands. At the end of the night the last of the flaming torches are thrown on to a fire. Bonfire society members then jump over the flames in a final salute to those put to death.

The Cafe
The Old Needlemakers
West Street
Lewes
East Sussex

Telephone: 01273 486258
Open: Monday to Saturday 9.30am-5.30pm

The Cafe, and a number of small craft shops, are located in converted Victorian factories. The old brick floors and beamed ceilings have been retained and an original well can be seen in the cellar.

The cafe is a popular meeting place for morning coffee, lunch and afternoon tea. There are delicious home made scones, quiches, cakes, biscuits and special salads as well as good coffee and a variety of teas.

Polly's Pantry
The Old Stables
Market Street
Lewes

Open: *Monday to Saturday 9am-*
            5.30pm
Parking: At rear

This tea shop is in a converted stable tucked behind displays of gifts made by local craftspeople. A good selection of home made cakes is on offer, the house speciality being a delicious orange and chocolate slice. At lunch time soup, ploughman's, sandwiches and daily specials give a wide variety of choice, and a take away service is available.

The teas, coffees and chutneys used in Polly's Pantry are also for sale.

LINDFIELD

Lindfield is one of the most delightful small towns (or large villages) in Sussex. It has a pond overlooked by a crescent of old cottages and a High Street lined by lime trees and full of interesting shops; even a violin maker can be found here. It has at least three dozen fine old houses in the High Street at the end of which stands a very nice old church like a full stop marking the end of the road. Just by the church is the charming 15th century Church Cottage, and Old Place, c1590.

Durrant's Coffee House
High Street
Lindfield
West Sussex

Owner: Mrs M Atmore
Parking: In street

This is a busy little drop-in tea shop in the heart of this picturesque village. Durrant's

Coffee House has a warm and welcoming ambience where the staff are very friendly. There is a good variety of home made cakes at reasonable prices, plus delicious scones and tea cakes. And excellent meals are served at lunch time.

Eve's Tea Room
Past and Present
64 High Street
Lindfield
West Sussex

Telephone: 01444 483117
Open: 9.30am-5pm Monday to
Saturday; 11m-5pm Sunday
Owner Mary Elizabeth Robertson
Parking: In street

This tiny tea room (it seats only 15) is at the back of Past and Present a well known centre for antiques.You have to find your way through this treasure trove of a shop and you need time to browse. Much of the stock spills over into the tea room, where antique mirrors and pictures hang on the walls.

The tea room staff are all jolly and chatty and everyone joins in with the conversation. It is a happy haven of scrumptious home made cakes and freshly baked scones. You can choose from six blends of tea, sold by the pot. If coffee is your tipple your cup will be refilled if you are eating here. At midday there are light snacks and a takeaway service for those who cannot spare the time to sit. At times Eve's has a very cosmopolitan atmosphere when foreign dealers combine buying with a cream tea.

LITLINGTON

Litlington Tea Gardens
Litlington
East Sussex

Telephone: 01323 870222
Owner: Shirley Barrett
Open: 11am-5.30pm daily April to
October
Parking: In large car park

Along the country roads leading to Litlington, near Alfriston, there are warnings to go slowly as toads may be crossing!

Established more than 150 years ago in an unspoilt corner of the Cuckmere Valley, the tea gardens are believed to be the oldest in Sussex. There are lawns set with tables and chairs as well as little wooden pavilions around the perimeter that are smothered with climbing plants affording a more private place to take tea and giving shelter in inclement weather. The gardens have many rare trees, including an Indian bean tree and an ancient ginkgo. There is a selection of teas to chose from such as Assam, Lapsang Souchong, herbal and fruit tea. All the cakes are home made and the set teas include English Tea (tea and round of cucumber sandwiches); Garden Cream Tea (tea, one scone, cream, jam, butter and cake); and Litlington Cream Tea (two scones, cream, jam, and butter). From noon to 2.30pm lunch is served. A board gives the daily menu and there are always salads and jacket potatoes available. There is a large mulberry tree that drops its luscious fruit all over the lawn in autumn giving a free feast to the birds, wild life and small children who delight in finding the berries.

MAYFIELD

The High Street that runs along a ridge of the High Weald has been almost unchanged for centuries. It has an array of fine old buildings in timber, brick and stone. The views in this area are beautiful and even the car park (free) behind the High Street has a panoramic view over meadows and distant hills.

The Church of St Dunstan was recorded in 960 as being a wooden structure. This was replaced in the 13th century by a stone building. The fire that swept through the town in 1389 left only the west end and tower intact, but the church was restored and embellished over the passing years. Inside St Dunstan is depicted in a stained glass lancet window which may be covered, but it is possible to pull the curtain to one side to take a peak.

St Dunstan was Archbishop of Canterbury from 960 until about 988. He was an artist and a blacksmith, and he wrote the first Coronation service for the crowning of English monarchs.

Legend has it that while working at his forge he was confronted by a beautiful young woman who tried to lure him away, but as she moved he saw a cloven hoof protruding from beneath her skirt. With a quick movement Dunstan picked up the red hot tongs from the fire and pinched the Devil's nose. With one leap the Devil sprang to Tunbridge Wells where he cooled his sore nose in the chalybeate spring (in The Pantiles). From that day to this the water has taken on its curious metallic flavour.

April Cottage
West Street
Mayfield
East Sussex

Telephone: 01435 872160
Open: 3pm-5.30pm daily
Owner: Barbara Powner

Open only to serve teas, April Cottage has a huge fireplace that takes up the whole of one wall. On chilly, dismal days the fire dances brightly giving off its warm glow and comfort. The tables, chairs and settles are all of dark oak while the walls are adorned with hand stitched tapestries.

Mrs Powner offers set teas, ranging from traditional Sussex Cream Tea, consisting of two scones, two types of home made jam, butter and clotted cream with pot of tea, to Small Cake Tea which has three cakes included in the price, together with tea or coffee. For those on special diets, Mrs Powner will try to serve food to suit and for anyone not able to eat the cakes all at once she will offer a bag to take home the remainder. Mobile 'phones are banned in April Cottage.

MIDHURST

This little town's quaintly named Knockhundred Row has two possible explanations. The first is that it was possible to 'knock-up' (muster) 100 men from the residents to defend the town should trouble arise. The second is that when the stock market was in the market square sheep would be held in flocks in this street which, being around a corner, was out of sight of the auction. As the sale progressed 100 knocks were made on the wall of the corner house to alert the drover to bring the next 100 sheep from Knockhundred Row and up into the market.

The Coffee Pot
Knockhundred Market
Knockhundred Row
Midhurst
West Sussex

Open: Monday to Saturday 9.30am-5pm;
*   Sunday 2.30pm-5.30pm*
Parking: In North Street car park

The Coffee Pot is in an old converted bar loft above Knockhundred Market, where there are a variety of small shops including a book seller, a florist and a china shop. The roof beams form an interesting feature and the rooms are pleasantly furnished with pine tables and chairs. The selection of teas includes Sussex Blend, herbal and speciality teas, and there is a good selection of cakes and scones. At midday a wide range of savoury snacks, salads and sandwiches may be enjoyed.

Ye Olde Tea Shoppe
North Street
Midhurst
West Sussex

Telephone: 01730 813481
Open: 10am to 5.30pm daily
Owners: Ian and Jackie Dummer

The most enormous teapot sits in the window of this olde worlde tea shop to advertise to all who pass by the nature of the business within. Many old beams give this building, which is believed to date as far back as 1545, a welcoming charm. Teas served here include Assam, China, Darjeeling and Earl Grey and they may be enjoyed with crumpets, teacakes, scones and scrumptious home made cakes.

HG Wells is thought to have lodged at this house while a pupil of the Midhurst Grammar School.

West Street Cafe
Midhurst Walk
West Street
Midhurst
West Sussex

Telephone: *01730 815085*
Open: *9am-5pm Monday to Saturday*
Owner: *Peter Crawford*
Parking: *In nearby car park*

West Street Cafe is at the end of a little arcade off West Street, not far from the car park in Grange Road. It is a friendly small place with an artisan feel from the local works of art and craft on sale nearby. The owner plays very good music (low in tone and not intrusive) and quite often it is jazz, Peter being a jazz musician himself. It is just the place to pop into for a light bite, where you can order such delights as boiled eggs with soldiers, toasted tea cakes and buttered crumpets.

Tea is served in a silver pot the choice being from blends of Assam, Dajeeling, Earl Grey or peppermint.

The Angel Hotel
North Street
Midhurst
West Sussex

Telephone: *01730 812412*
Owner: *Peter Crawford*

The Angel Hotel is a 16th century building located in the main thoroughfare of North Street. It was famous as the principal coaching inn until late in the 19th century. On the first floor you will find many of the original features in what was once the local court room (now mainly used for conferences). The hotel has a medieval walled garden where you can take tea by arrangement.

PATCHAM

The Coach House Tearoom
Old London Road
Patcham
Brighton
East Sussex

Telephone: 01273 553243
Open: Tuesday to Sunday (closed on
*   winter Sundays)*
Owner: Mrs Hawley
Parking: On street. Disabled access

The Coach House Tearoom was, as its name suggests, an old coach house complete with tall doors at the entrance and cobbled walls which make a appropriate backdrop for the horse harnesses and coachman's whips that are hung around them. Also on display are paintings (for sale) by local artists. There is a lovely garden with sheltered patio that is a popular place to sit on a warm day.

The delicious cream teas consist of two large scones, butter, cream and jam with a pot of tea. There is also a good selection of cakes, the speciality of the house being the chocolate apricot meringue. A variety of teas includes Assam, Ceylon, China and Darjeeling. Or there is coffee for those who prefer it.

Mrs Hawley delights in serving fresh and wholesome food offering a reasonably priced choice of light lunches that include jacket potatoes and quiches. The tea room is fully licensed and small parties can be catered for.

Patcham Village has long since been engulfed by Brighton but if time permits stroll up Church Hill past the quaint old cottages to the green in front of the church. Not so long ago it was a large pond and elderly residents still talk of the spring nights when as children they were unable to sleep because of the croaking of the many frogs that congregated there. At the top of the green (still known as the pond) you will see what was the longest tythe barn in Sussex (now converted into houses). Opposite this is what is believed to be one of the oldest dovecotes in existence with walls three feet thick and 550 nesting holes.

PEVENSEY

Castle Cottage Tea Room
Pevensey Castle
Pevensey
East Sussex

Telephone: 01323 460382
Open: Daily 10am-6pm April to
*   October; 10am-4pm*
*   December; Wednesday to*
*   November, January to March*
Owner: Janet Southouse

Castle Cottage was built during Victorian times and nestles up against the outer wall of the original Roman fortress. William the Conqueror later ordered that a castle be constructed within the old Roman fort. The remains of both are open to the public. The cottage, restored by English Heritage in 1990, contains the local Tourist Information Centre and is a thriving tea room and licensed restaurant.

Janet Southouse offers an inviting selection of cream teas, home made cakes, scones, biscuits, and shortbread. For lunch there is a choice of two or three baked daily specials, fresh sandwiches or a hearty soup. Also available are ploughman's lunches or a Cottage Luncheon of home cooked beef or ham with a crusty roll, pickles and salad.

On sunny summer days it is very enjoyable to dine on the patio or in the garden, which is quite sheltered. Traditional English fare is served in the evening (Thursday, Friday and Saturday) and we recommend that you book for this as it is a very popular evening venue.

The excellent food is from local suppliers - fish from Pevensey Bay and fruit from nearby farms all beautifully presented and served.

POLEGATE

Gibby's Cottage Tea Rooms
Jevington Road
Polegate
East Sussex

Telephone: 01323 482484
Open: 10am-5.30pm Tuesday to
       Sunday and bank holidays
Owner: David Harris
Parking: On site

Gibby's, established in 1926, lies in a fold in the South Downs between Wannock and Jevington. The black and white house is surrounded by gardens full of roses, shrubs and trees making this a pleasant stop on a sunny afternoon to enjoy a cup of tea, and watch the world go by. Here you will also find a small collection of unusual chickens that amuse children and adults alike. This is really more of a tea garden than a tea room, with the tables and chairs set outside protected from the sun by parasols, although the tea rooms make a good inside retreat on wet or cold days.

David Harris treats his clients as friends making every effort to please. He will go to great lengths to cater for any special need, given two days' notice. For those who are allergic to wheat flour he stocks a special dietary flour enabling the staff to make dishes to suit.

Here chocolate roulade is top of the popularity list. This is a deliciously light cake made with lots of eggs and cocoa, rolled up full of chocolate mousse and double cream, and it is closely followed by toasted hazel nut meringue filled with apricots and cream. There are traditional cream teas on offer and a good selection of home made cakes of all types together with light lunches such as poached eggs and a choice of ice creams. For a more substantial meal the menu offers steak pie, gammon steaks and fresh salmon.

ROTTINGDEAN

Rottingdean is an English Downland village by the sea on Brighton's eastern border. In the years when it was an isolated farming community much smuggling was reputed to have gone on and Rottingdean gained a name for its illicit trade.

The area around the picturesque pond has inspired painters for years, and many famous writers, artists and eminent people having made their homes in this quaint village.

Rudyard Kipling lived in The Elms, a large beautiful house overlooking the pond, but moved away to Burwash when fame overtook his privacy.

When in Rottingdean saunter around the village sampling the atmosphere of the galleries, tea rooms and shops. Visit its old church of St Margaret where you can see the bullet holes in the walls made by a French raiding party, or walk up Beacon Hill to sit and take refreshment at the small cafe by the windmill.

The Trellis
39 High Street
Rottingdean
East Sussex

Telephone: 01273 302837
Open: 10am-7.30pm daily except Wednesday
Owner: Mary Venturi
Parking: On sea front

This interesting 17th century restaurant in the busy High Street was at one time the meeting place for the girls from Roedean. Pauline remembers being taken there as a child and being fascinated by the children of the rich and famous, tucking into cream cakes with voracious appetites.

There is a sun-trap courtyard garden outside where you can while away the time amidst the colourful pots of flowers and gay sun shades. The Trellis specialises in traditional home cooked meals and delicious Sussex cream teas as well as serving coffee, lunches and dinners. This is a convenient place for disabled people being on the flat and with fairly easy access.

Olde Cottage Tea Rooms and
   Restaurant
62/64 High Street
Rottingdean
East Sussex

Telephone: 01273 303426
Open: 10am-7pm Wednesday to
            Sunday; other days by
            arrangement

This delightful tea shop was built in 1589 as two fishermen's cottages with secret underground passages used by smugglers. The original beams and stone floors can still be seen. The friendly ghost of a Mrs Mockford, who lived here in the late 19th century, is reputed to appear occasionally. Her descendants still live in the village.

Olde Cottage has three low-beamed dining rooms, seating 50. At the back there are tea gardens stocked with shrubs, climbing roses and many varieties of flowers. There is easy ramp access for the disabled, inside and out.

The tea rooms sell a large selection of home made jams, marmalades and lemon curd, locally packed teas, honey, home made fudge, home made cakes and scones to eat on the premises or take away. Lunches and light snacks are served all day.

RYE

Simon the Pieman
Lion Street
Rye
East Sussex

Telephone: 01797 222207
Open: All day Tuesday to Saturday and
            Sunday afternoon
Owner: Mr J Layfield

This is the oldest established tea room in Rye, situated a few doors down from the church and it is all that remains of the old Red Lion Inn that was burned down in 1972. The tea room still has the original fireplace that dates from the 16th century and old beams from which hang an array of Sussex trugs. On the walls are old photographs of Rye in days gone by.

Teas served are Indian and Earl Grey, the choice of cakes are of the most wicked sort - doughnuts and coffee meringues that are filled to order, chocolate eclairs, cream slices, passion cake, treacle tart and toasted tea cakes plus a whole selection of fancies are displayed in the shop window to entice you in.

For lunch fresh fish and chips is a popular choice, as are chicken and mushroom pie and quiche.

Cobbles Tea Rooms
1 Hylands Yards
Rye
East Sussex

Telephone: *01797 225962*
Open: *Daily 10.30am-5.30pm*
Owner: *Jennifer Wall*
Parking: *In town car parks*

Tucked into the corner of this alleyway is a delightful little tea shop started in 1952. The old oak beams and lace tablecloths on the round tables give a homely and friendly feel, echoed by the warm welcome from the staff. The china on the tables is blue willow pattern, and tea is served in dear little teapots for one.

Twenty different varieties of tea are to be found here; the house blend, a three star graded Kenyan, is the most popular, but among the others are Oolong Formosa, Rose, Pouchong and Earl Grey. All the cakes are home made with carrot cake being the house speciality. Locally produced fruit and vegetables are included in the menu wherever possible and Willets Farm Ice Cream is served in unusual assorted flavours such as honey and nut and vanilla and ginger.

Swan Cottage Tea Rooms
41 The Mint
Rye
East Sussex

Telephone: 01797 222423
Open: Summer daily 10.30am-4.30pm;
winter daily 10.30am-4pm
(closed Tuesdays)
Owner: Mr Beecroft

Timbered Swan Cottage, thought to date from 1420, has seen a number of uses over the centuries, from an inn to a wet fish and bloater shop. The old oak beams and low ceilings invite you in. There is a small front parlour for the smokers and an inner sanctum for non smokers. The walls are decorated by Mr Beecroft with embroidery that he has painstakingly done himself, and the little round tables are covered in pink cloths.

The Swan is renowned for its chocolate eclairs and strawberry gateaux, which may be served with either the special house blend or Earl Grey tea. The cream tea comprises two scones, cream, butter, jam and pot of tea. Swan Tea (for the hungry) consists of sandwiches plus the cream tea.

At lunch time the menu offers a good choice including quiches, jacket potato with various fillings, vegetarian dishes and Welsh rarebit. At the back is a garden that can be approached via Cinque Port Street as well as through the tea shop. The garden has a plentiful supply of tables and chairs to use on warm sunny days and children and dogs are welcome at the Swan.

STANMER

Stanmer is a model village set in a beautiful park. Although owned (and probably saved) by Brighton Corporation, it has retained a unique atmosphere of times past. A compact little unit, the village has a working farm, church, pond, cottages and the big house. Stanmer House, largely created by the Pelham family in the 18th century, is believed to be one of the first to have piped water.

The Tea Shop
Stanmer Stores
Stanmer
Brighton

Telephone: 01273 604041
Open: Daily 9am to 9pm
Owners: Phil Carless and Jan Cameron
Parking: In village street

This tea shop is part of the village shop where you are surrounded by the necessities of life from all manner of foodstuffs to stamps and postcards. There is also a restaurant/tea room in the adjoining cottage as well as tables and chairs set out on the forecourt. Here cream teas can be enjoyed as can traditional roast dinners (weekends only) with lovely old puddings such as spotted dick and treacle pudding. Booking is essential for the restaurant, particularly at Christmas time.

STORRINGTON

Willow Tea Room and Garden
Pulborough Road
Storrington
West Sussex

Telephone: 01903 742600
Open: 11am-5.30pm Tuesday to
*   Sunday and bank holidays*
Owners: David and Nicole Weston
Parking: Outside

A friendly atmosphere is to be found here and on a warm summer's day what could be better than to sit in an English garden by a pond eating a traditional afternoon tea? At Willow Tea Room there are sumptuous cream teas to enjoy with a very tempting display of coffee and walnut cake, wholemeal fruit and rich cherry cakes as well as freshly baked fruit pies. The blackboard lists the day's main dishes such as soups, wholefood and vegetarian dishes. Light snacks like buck rarebit, ham and cheese ploughman's lunches or a choice of omelettes are also available. Sundays bring traditional roasts served with fresh vegetables from local sources.

Weeping willows are believed to have been introduced to England via a basket from Turkey. In the 18th century Lady Suffolk was sent a gift of a basket of 'figgs' from her friend, the poet Alexander Pope, who planted 'twiggs' from the basket. The twigs grew into trees that we know as weeping willows, says the old story.

Paulines
Church Street
Storrington
West Sussex

Telephone: *01903 744802*
Open: *9.30am-3.30pm Monday to Friday, April to*
October 9.30am-2pm Monday to Friday, November to March, closed Sundays
and bank holidays

These little tea rooms are tucked at the back of the shops on the right hand side going up Church Street in Storrington - just the place to pop into when a cup of tea or coffee is required to revive your spirits when out shopping or doing business in the area.

Here you will find a good pot of tea and a selection of home baked cakes on offer. The food is prepared right in front of your eyes as Pauline's kitchen is set between the two rooms and open to view. A selection of filled rolls is available at lunch time. There is also a sheltered garden to sit out in on warm days.

The South Downs rise a mile or so from Storrington and from Chanctonbury Ring there is a panoramic view over Sussex, Kent,

Surrey, and Hampshire. Before the hurricane of October 16 1987 devastated Chactonbury Ring, it was a magnificent stand of beech trees crowning the hill top. It was planted by Charles Goring of Wiston when he was a schoolboy, about 250 years ago.

He tended his seedlings every day by taking water up the hill, and he went on to plant many more trees on the Downs from Washington to Steyning.

Left, Chanctonbury Ring

TICEHURST

Pashley Manor Gardens
Ticehurst
Nr Wadhurst
East Sussex

Telephone: *01580 200692*
Open: *11am-5pm April to September,*
Tuesday, Wednesday,
Thursday and Saturday and
bank holidays
Owners: *Mr and Mrs J A Sellick*
Parking: *Car park, admission charge to gardens*

Pashley Manor was the home of the de Passele family until 1453 when the estate was purchased and owned until 1543 by the Boleyn family. It is thought that during her childhood Anne, the second wife of Henry VIII, stayed here. Sir Thomas May demolished the original house when he bought it from the Boleyns, and built the house you see today, although alterations to the facade were made by later members of his family in about 1720. It was then that the garden was established.

Pashley Manor prides itself on its delicious food with the afternoon teas being taken on the terrace under colonial style sun shades on fine days. The full afternoon tea comprises scones, cakes and biscuits with a pot of tea. Cream from a local Jersey herd is used in the manor's delicious cream teas.

For lunch, home made soup with granary bread is on the menu, as are ploughman's lunches with home made pickles, large salads fresh from the garden with cheeses, smoked salmon pate or chicken pate. Filter coffee and soft drinks are also on offer.

The Tea Shop
1 The High Street
Ticehurst
East Sussex

Telephone: 01580 200015
Open: 10am-5pm Monday to Saturday,
              10am-2pm Wednesday
Owners: Peter and Joan Langrish
Parking   On street

The Tea Shop in picturesque Ticehurst is in hop country, where many delightful oast houses (now converted to homes) are reminders of the flourishing hop gardens of old.

It is furnished with oak chairs and tables that are pleasantly laid with floral china (the tea pots come complete with tea cosies) while the walls are adorned with pictures that are for sale.

Here can be found a selection of home made cakes and tea breads together with the traditional cream tea comprising two scones with butter, jam and cream plus pot of tea.

Home cooked ham is offered in a variety of dishes including salads, buck rarebit or toasted muffins topped with bacon, egg and tomato make a very pleasant savoury snack.

Apart from tea or coffee the drinks available are honey and cinnamon in hot milk, good on chilly days, or citrus punch sold by the jug, excellent to quench a thirst in warmer weather.

UCKFIELD

Barnsgate Manor Vineyard
Tea Room
Herons Ghyll
Nr Uckfield
East Sussex

Telephone: 01825 713366
Open: Daily from 10am
Parking: On site

This tea room enjoys the most beautiful panoramic views reaching far beyond the vineyard to the Sussex Weald. It has a Mediterranean feel with a stencilled grape frieze appropriate to the vineyard. There is also a licensed restaurant which has an excellent varied menu that caters for all tastes. Bookings may be taken for functions.

The vineyard offers plenty to occupy a family, not only a trail to follow with donkeys and lamas to see en route, but also a wine and gift shop, plus guided tours by arrangement.

Herons Ghyll, on the A26 between Crowborough and Uckfield, was given its name by the Victorian author Coventry Patmore, who bought a small estate by the name of Puckstay, in 1866. There he built a house (named Temple Grove today) on the site of the former house. The Patmore family left the house in 1875 to live in Hastings and the original estate, which included what is now Barnsgate, has since been split up.

UPPARK

Uppark
South Harting
West Sussex

Telephone: 01730 825415
Open: March 31 to October 31 Sunday to
             Thursday, tea room noon-5.30pm;
             house 1pm-5pm; garden and exhibition
             noon-5.30pm
Owner: The National Trust
Parking: In car park

Set in the old kitchen, this tea room is furnished with green wooden tables and chairs complemented by green and stone coloured pottery. The floor is covered with coir matting while from the high ceiling hang three large lantern lights. Presiding over the whole room is a huge clock. From the windows there are lovely views of the gardens. Choose from Indian or Earl Grey Tea, which is served by the pot. There is a daily changing selection of home made cakes and shortbreads to try, or the cream tea of scone, jam and cream with pot of tea. The light lunches include excellent home made soup with crisp rolls and jacket potatoes with various fillings.

The tea room is connected to the house via a system of underground tunnels and flights of steps so in days gone by servants could take the food to the dining room without being seen by anyone above stairs.

Uppark House was built about 1690 and is set high on the Downs, with exceptionally fine views reaching to the Solent. It is surrounded by gardens designed by Humphrey Repton. Emma, the future Lady Hamilton, Admiral Lord Nelson's inamorata, was a fifteen year old dancing girl, with a child, when she was taken to Uppark to become the mistress of Sir Harry Featherstonhaugh. Emma was subsequently passed to Charles Greville, and then Sir William Hamilton, whom she eventually married.

On August 30, 1989 a fire raged through the house causing considerable damage, but fortunately nearly all the antique furniture and paintings were rescued by staff, fire-fighters and visitors. Today it has been completely restored and an exhibition centre shows the restoration from devastation to the beautiful house that has risen from the ashes.

WADHURST

Wealden Wholefoods
High Street
Wadhurst
East Sussex

WEALDEN WHOLEFOODS Café-Gallery

Telephone: 01892 783065
Open: 9am-5.15pm
               Monday to Saturday
Owners: Wealden Wholefood Co-operative Ltd
Parking: In street

This rustic tea shop is at the back of Wealden Wholefood and it has a small garden to sit in on sunny days. Here is to be found a large selection of teas from traditional Kenyan to the many speciality teas such as peppermint or cinnamon and apple. The tea is served in delightful little floral tea pots with cups to match. Coffee comes in individual cafeterias and is an organic Mexican variety; even the hot chocolate served here is organic.

  As the Wholefood name suggests everything that can be is organically produced and most is vegetarian also. At lunch time there is a selection of home made soups and vegetarian dishes to enjoy. The shop has amazing array of organically grown produce and foods supplied by members of the co-operative, plus a huge selection of herbal remedies and aromatherapy oils.

WALBERTON

Beam Ends
Hedgers Hill
Nr Walberton
West Sussex

Telephone: 01243 551254
Open: 11am-5.30pm (not Monday)
               May to September;
               11am-5.30pm Thursday to Sunday,
               October, March, April; 11am-5pm,
               weekends remaining months
Owners: Rick and Coral Botting
Parking: In grounds

If you want to get the feel of how it would be to live in an old thatched cottage do go to have tea at Beam Ends. The owners Rick and Coral like to think of their customers as 'visiting us in our home' and this is exactly the feel of the place. When we visited there was a lovely warm fire and some comfortable armchairs with a cat curled up asleep on one. The cakes served here are delicious and are cooked by Coral; banana and walnut cakes, apple pies (melt in your mouth) and bakewell tarts are her speciality. You will have a choice of many loose leaf teas, served in china cups from china pots.

On summer days it's lovely to sit outside in the quiet garden which has spectacular views across the dean to Binstead Church.

At Beam Ends you can have a light lunch with a special dish of the day, or (with 24 hours' notice) a full scale Sunday roast lunch to which you can take your own wine if you wish. There are also themed dinners - call for details.

WINCHELSEA

The Tea Tree
12 High Street
Winchelsea
East Sussex

Telephone: 01797 226102
Open: 10am-6pm Wednesday to
Monday; closed January
Owner: Wendy Harris
Parking: In street

This is one of the very best tea shops in Sussex. Its warm and friendly atmosphere makes it just the place to relax with a good pot of tea. There are beamed ceilings, an inglenook fireplace and a wood burning stove which, on winter days, glows merrily. The windows are draped with pretty floral curtains and the tables dressed with matching cloths. On warm sunny days there is a small paved garden full of flowers to sit in while enjoying your tea or coffee.

The choice of teas and coffees is unrivalled, the tea being served in elegant teapots each with its own infuser while the coffee comes in individual cafetierres. Cakes are all home baked with the 18 Carat Carrot Cake being a speciality. At lunch time soup such as corn chowder features on the daily changing menu which always has a vegetarian choice along with salads and jacket potatoes, all served on blue and white china.

An area of the shop is given over to selling loose teas and coffees. Dozens of varieties line the shelves and if they don't have your favourite in stock they will do their best to obtain it for you. People come from all over the world to seek out this tea shop and to take an ample stock of their chosen blends home.

WORTHING

Highdown Tea Rooms
Littlehampton Road
Worthing
West Sussex

Telephone: 01903 246984
Open: Daily 10am-4pm winter;
*   10am-6pm summer*
Owner: Robina Dove

This homely and charming restaurant is situated right next to Highdown Chalk Gardens and has ample parking right outside making it ideal for those who are disabled. The interior is welcoming and the staff friendly and helpful. Food is good, wholesome and nicely presented at very reasonable prices. There is a wonderful selection of cakes which are baked on the premises, the restaurant also sells a variety of craft items and paintings. On warm summer days, you can sit outside and watch a multitude of wild birds come and pick crumbs up from around the tables.

The unique chalk gardens were created by Sir Frederick and Lady Stern who worked for 50 years to prove that plants would grow on chalk. The gardens are in a chalk pit overlooking the Downs, where there is little soil, irregular ground and very unfavourable conditions for growth. Sir Frederick was an eminent research biologist who specialised in plant cells and culture techniques. He conducted experiments in his laboratory at Highdown and the results of his hybridisations can be seen in the garden. The rare and beautiful plants come from all over the world, and include lilies, magnolia, and wisteria, azaleas and rhododendrons, roses and peonies. The garden is owned and managed by Worthing Borough Council.

FOREST ROW

The Hybrid Tea
Wych Cross
Forest Row
East Sussex

Telephone: 01342 822705
Open: 10am-5pm Monday to Saturday
Parking: On site

The Hybrid Tea is situated in the grounds of Wych Cross Nursery and Garden Centre. It is a tiny bright and cheerful place where the staff are helpful, the cakes home made, prices reasonable, cream teas delightful and coffee good. The selection of snacks include soup with a roll and ploughman's lunches.

NATIONAL TRUST PROPERTIES WITH TEA ROOMS

NYMANS GARDENS: These beautiful gardens contain rare plants from around the world. There are romantic ruins, a walled garden, woodland walks and a sunken garden. Nymans is on the B214 at Handcross, four and a half miles south of Crawley, just off the London-Brighton M23/A23. Open daily, March 1 to November 2, 11am to 6pm or sunset; closed Monday and Tuesday (except bank holiday Mondays). Winter opening Saturday and Sunday only, noon to 4pm. The licensed tea room serves a light lunch menu as well as teas between 11am and 5pm. A restricted menu is in operation from November to February, but the tea room is open for Christmas lunches. Telephone 01444 400321.

PETWORTH HOUSE: A 17th century house, set in a 700 acre deer park landscaped by Capability Brown, holding a fine collection of paintings and carvings. It is in the centre of Petworth (A272/A283) and the car park is well signposted. Open March 28 to November 2 daily, 1pm to 5.30pm, except Thursday and Friday (open Good Friday). The licensed tea room serves coffee, light lunches and teas between noon and 5pm. Christmas lunches may be booked. Telephone: 01798 352207. **PETWORTH PARK** is open all year, free entry, 8am to sunset, except June 27-29, when it closes at noon.

SHEFFIELD PARK GARDENS: A superb garden laid out by Capability Brown in the 18th century. The four lakes are linked by waterfalls and cascades and the collection of rare trees and shrubs make this a garden full of interest at any time of year. The gardens are mid-way between East Grinstead and Lewes, five miles north west of Uckfield on the A272 (between A272/A22) half a mile from Sheffield Park station (Bluebell Railway). Open March 28 to November 16, Tuesday to Sunday, and bank holiday Mondays, 11am to 6pm, or sunset if earlier. Winter opening November 19 to December 21, Wednesday to Sunday, 11am to 4pm; March, weekends only, 11am to 6pm. Telephone: 01823 790231. The tea room is not National Trust but it is of a good standard and situated close to the gardens.

WAKEHURST PLACE: Managed as an outpost of the Royal

Botanical Gardens of Kew, this wonderful garden is laid out in sections showing the plants from various regions of the world growing in authentic habitats. Exotic plants thrive in the Southern Hemisphere garden and the Himalayan Glade, while the plants of the Northern Hemisphere grow in profusion in other areas. It is one and a half miles north west of Ardingly on the B2028. Open daily all year (except December 25 and January 1) November to the end of January 10am to 4pm. February and October, 10am to 5pm. March, 10am to 6pm. April to the end of September, 10am to 7pm. The mansion closes one hour before the gardens. Telephone: 01444 894066. For refreshment there is a fully licensed restaurant (not National Trust) serving a selection of home made cakes, salads, hot and cold snacks and full meals.

TEA SPECIALISTS

TRADEWINDS, The Riverside Centre, High Street, Lewes.
Tradewinds is a shop that sells nothing but tea and coffee, mainly in loose form so you can buy as much or as little as you wish. There are more than sixty different varieties of tea from all over the world - Japan, India, Formosa, Ceylon, China and Kenya. They come as black tea, green tea, white tea or special teas, such as Lapsang Souchong (produced by withering the leaves over open pine fires). Herbal and fruit teas are also sold here as well as local blends such as Lewes Five O'clock Tea and Lewes 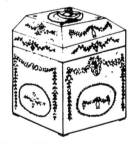 Bonfire Tea, which doesn't have to be reserved for November the Fifth. Although only a small shop on the upper floor of the Riverside Centre, it is so brim full of fascinating things that you need time to peruse the shelves before making your selection. Telephone: 01273 488244.

THE SUSSEX TEA COMPANY, PO Box 66, Uckfield, TN22 3AN
This is a mail order service that supplies good quality tea either loose or in tea bags. Sussex Tea, the company's flagship tea, is first class tea

from Kenya. Others available are:

Assam: A full bodied tea selected for its full rich malty flavour

Darjeeling: Finest of the Indian teas with a delicate muscantel flavour from the foothills of the Himalayas.

Lapsang Souchong: Classic large black leaf, offers a fine syrup-smoky flavour.

Keemun: The old imperial traditional tea rich in aromatics with a subtle sappy taste.

Jasmine: A mild flavoured China tea with a jasmine flower scent.

Earl Grey: Black China tea blended with oil of bergamont, believed to have been presented by a Chinese mandarin to the Earl.

Summer Cooler: Oil of cornflowers, mallow, tropicana, marigold and thistle blended with China tea (available April 1 to September 30).

Winter Warmer: China tea blended with orange peel, cloves and almonds (available September 1 to April 30).

The company also stocks a selection of delicious fruit tea infusions that include Berry Fruit Cocktail and Apple Viennese.

Telephone: 01825 732601; Fax: 01825 732730.

We hope you have enjoyed this little book. We apologise if we have missed out your favourite tea shop and would welcome a letter to let us know about it. Please write to Secret Sussex Tours Ltd, 1 Sunnyside Cottages, Rodmell, Nr Lewes, East Sussex BN7 3HA.

Joan Ellis and Pauline Cherry

THE AUTHORS' FAVOURITES

Here are the tea shops that Pauline and Joan return to again and again on their Secret Sussex Tours. The choice is personal, of course, and tea shop aficionados may enjoy drawing up their own lists of favourite places.

WEST SUSSEX

Amberley Castle	Amberley
Beam Ends	Walburton
Norton House	Henfield
Belinda's	Arundel
Burdocks	Billingshurst
Highdown Tea Rooms	Worthing
Willow Tea Room	Storrington
Mariners	Bosham
Eve's Tea Room	Lindfield
Seasons	Cuckfield

EAST SUSSEX

The Tea Tree	Winchelsea
Firle Place	Firle
Katie's Pantry	Hastings
The Swan	Rye
Badgers	Alfriston
The Pavilion	Eastbourne
Castle Cottage	Pevensey
Duddleswell Tea Rooms	Duddleswell
Knollys	Bodiam
The Queen Adelaide Tea Rooms	Brighton

TOP TEA SHOPS IN WEST SUSSEX

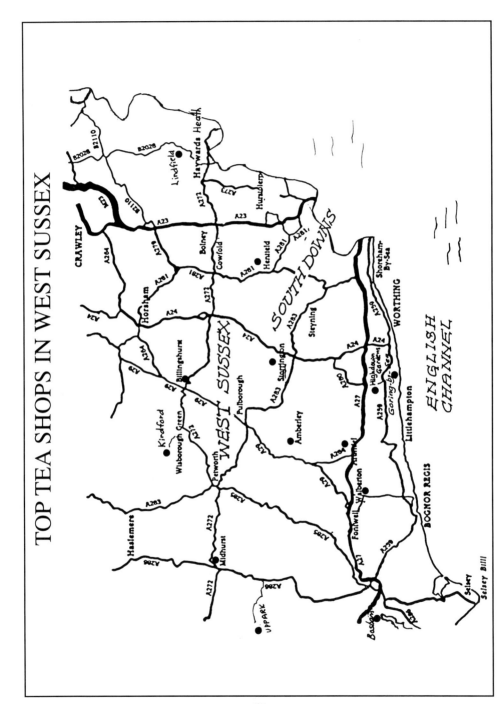

TOP TEA SHOPS IN EAST SUSSEX

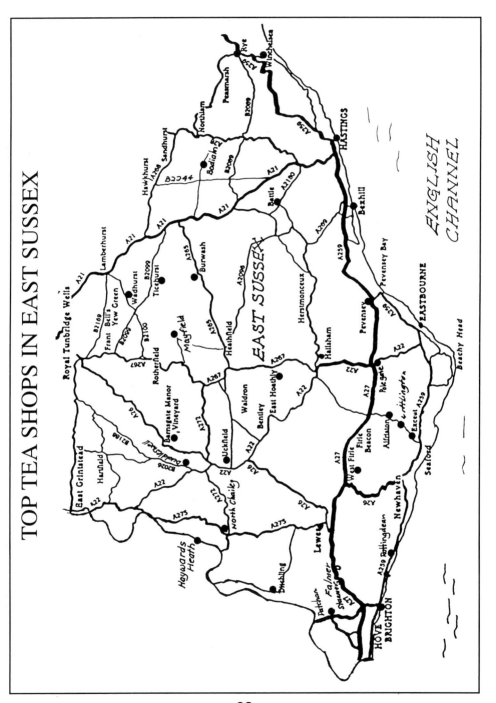

ABOUT THE AUTHORS

 PAULINE CHERRY was a technical illustrator in the School of Engineering and Applied Sciences at the University of Sussex for 21 years, and she has worked as a freelance illustrator and engraver. Most of the illustrations in this book were drawn by Pauline. Her work has been exhibited in the Louvre in Paris. Pauline has run her own tourism business, Sussex Chauffeur Guide, since 1989, taking visitors around Hidden Sussex.

JOAN ELLIS, a busy mother of two, helps her husband Roger with his building contracting business and also runs a bed and breakfast service. Joan has a great interest in local history and folklore. In 1996 Joan and Pauline set up Secret Sussex Tours Ltd, a company that provides specialist tours for overseas visitors. In its first year the business won a Tourism Award from Lewes Chamber of Commerce.

S.B. Publications publish a wide range of local interest books on Sussex and other counties in England. For a complete list write (inc. S.A.E.) to:- S.B. Publications, c/o 19 Grove Road, Seaford, East Sussex BN25 1TP.